ORACLE CARDS 101

A GUIDEBOOK TO UNDERSTANDING DIVINATION

SUNNY DAWN JOHNSTON

ORACLE CARDS 101

SDJ Productions LLC
4640 W. Redfield Road
Glendale, AZ 85306
www.sunnydawnjohnston.com

ISBN: 978-1-7324357-4-2

Cover Design by Kris Voelker Designs
Compiled by Deb McGowan
Interior Formatting & Design by Shanda Trofe

Printed in the United States of America.

DEDICATION

This book is dedicated to all souls that desire to connect even greater with the Spirit World.

CONTENTS

INTRODUCTION

I'm Sunny Dawn Johnston, and I am sooo excited to be "meeting" you. If you are reading this book, you are ready to learn how to use oracle cards to develop your intuition. Using oracle cards can benefit you and those you are connected to. Congratulations! You are embarking on an awesome journey and I am excited to be the one to guide and support you.

You see, I LOVE oracle cards. As a matter of fact, I have collected over 250 oracle card decks over the past 30+ years. My love affair started back at the age of 13, when I started using *Gong Hee Fot Choy* cards to help me connect with Spirit, look further within, and bring me peace of mind in a time where I didn't feel much peace (you know… teenager). Once a week (it said not to consult them more than that, so I didn't) my mom and I would get out the book & the cards and we would do readings. I remember always feeling relief afterwards. It was like I had received some counsel that had said to me "everything is going to be OK," and for a short time, it felt true. I didn't realize then, that I was actually receiving counsel and that my spirit was setting in motion an experience that I would not only use for myself but teach thousands of others how to use as well.

Fast forward a decade or so and oracle cards became not only a part of my life but a part of my daily spiritual practice. Picking a card for the day to focus my intention and energy on helped me to stay focused. As a stay-at-home mom, there were many times when I felt like I would lose my mind, but the intention I set in the morning would "remind" me of my true purpose or focus for the day.

About that time, a few new oracle cards were being produced. When angel cards came out, I fell in love all over again. They just felt so "right." It was shortly after that when I started offering oracle card readings myself. I started with Angel and Fairy card readings. They were the perfect doorway for me to begin my journey to OWNING my psychic abilities and learning to TRUST my intuition. Maybe you are just embarking on this path yourself. I believe learning how to use oracle cards and be intentional with the energy you use them in, can help support you in ways that can truly change your life. They've sure changed mine.

Oracles and divination tools have long been a part of history. For thousands of years, people have wanted to tune in and connect with the Spirit World and have used a variety of tools to do this. Whether you are new to Oracle Cards or have used them for years, there is always more to learn. I have discovered in my own life that being a student of the Oracle brings about the greatest learning, which in turn offers the opportunity for the greatest teaching.

As a teacher of spiritual development, mediumship and intuition for the past 20+ years and a student for over 35 years, I understand that people are different. They are in different places, have different levels of awareness, are on different vibrations, and have different comfort levels in trusting their intuition. We all must start somewhere, which is why I have compiled some of what I have learned over the years into this format. When using Oracle Cards, the biggest stumbling block I have encountered is the tendency to rely too heavily on the published guidebook, and not enough on your own intuition. What I have found is that using the included guidebook that comes with many decks is best used not as a crutch to depend on, but more as a support when you really need it.

Guidebooks are great to read when you first start using a new deck. It's fun to read the descriptions and get a sense of the deck. But we don't want to become dependent on them. Just like when you're learning to drive, you get to a point when driver's ed is over and it's time to let go of the manual and drive on your own… trusting your ability to do so. **Learning to trust your intuition helps you develop your innate connection to Spirit.** I promise, you will be guided, and YOU can do this!

Learning to listen to your own intuition and connecting to that guidance for yourself is so critical. If you're connected inward, you know where your true power lies … you know where the wisdom truly is. You know that you can rely on that connection – and you will always be able to do that. **Learning to TRUST your Intuition is one of the greatest gifts you can receive**. It is already innate. All it takes is some awareness and some practice. If you are ready to open up to your intuition, expand your awareness and tune into the oracles, read on!

This book offers you several ways to connect with your Oracle Card deck, including how to prepare your deck and clear your cards, ethics for oracle card readers as well as several card spreads that are unique. I've also added tips that will help you to truly expand and grow your intuitive muscle and get that trust in yourself and Spirit stronger. I know you are ready, or you wouldn't be reading this book. So, grab your cards and let's get started.

Welcome to the Journey –

With so much LOVE and Light to you,

SDJ (aka Sunny Dawn Johnston)

Preparing Your Deck for Use

These are steps I take to prepare my decks. If you already have your own practice, follow your own guidance as to what you may want to incorporate. If you are new to oracle cards, I offer this information to help you with a starting point. Either way, take what feels right and fits for you and leave the rest.

Clear the Space

It is really important that the space you use to do your readings is cleared first. Have a clear space physically, mentally, emotionally, and energetically. Clean up the physical environment around you if it feels cluttered. Create a positive vibrational space: open the windows, clear the space using **sage** or **VibeRaiser**, gather a couple of crystals, or light a candle and/or incense. Surround yourself with the things that raise your vibration and make you feel connected to Spirit.

Clear Your Mind and Body

Don't read oracle cards when you're under the influence of alcohol or any other addictive substance. Having a clear mind and body is important because it allows you to really tune into the guidance of your intuition and the messages your angels, guides, and ascended masters are sending. Even though readings can be fun, they are serious as well. You want your frequency to be high and your life force energy up-beat... you don't want your energy to be in a lower vibration... which then affects everything else.

Raise Your Vibration

Having high-energy is a great way to start. Turn on some spiritual music, ground yourself, meditate, pray, light some incense, breathe in deeply. Do whatever it is that YOU need to do to open yourself up and con-nect... do that!

Invite Your Angels, Guides, Deceased Loved Ones, and Ascended Masters (Your Spirit Team)

Call in your Angels, Guides, Deceased Loved Ones, and Ascended Masters in to be with you and guide you throughout the reading. I like to ask Spirit/Divine/Source Energy/God of your understanding to allow me to connect with the person I am reading for (or myself), and their (your) Spirit Team for the highest greatest good. I ask that messages of love, guidance, and sup-port come to me and through me for the highest good of all concerned. I also ask Archangel Michael to help me to protect and/or maintain my energy so that I can be a clear channel for the person I am reading for (or for myself). This will also help you to hold your own energy so that you don't absorb the energy of others around you… physical or non-physical.

Infuse Your New Oracle Cards

To begin, open your new deck and read the introduction to the cards by the author. This is usually found in the accompanying guidebook or insert. Once you have done that, follow each of the above steps to prepare your deck. Now comes the fun part: infusing your new cards!

Once you have received your cards, I believe it is important to infuse each of them with YOUR energy. Although it is likely that you will be using your cards to do readings for others, not just yourself, you want to have your energy imbued into your deck for greater clarity when connecting with your Spirit Team.

Pick one card and look at that card. Sense the energy flowing from the card. Tune into the light and the message that the card brings to you. Observe how the cards feels to you. Notice any messages you might hear when you connect with the card. Read the words on the card. Just be present with the card for a few seconds or even a minute or so as you breathe in the energy of the card with nice deep breaths. Once you feel complete, go to the next card, doing this with each card in the deck. Tune into the energy and what each card represents to you and for you. This is how you consecrate this deck and make it a trustworthy tool to support you and those you read for.

Give Thanks

After you have imbued your new card deck with your awesome energy then I believe it is so important to give thanks for the opportunities, wisdom, and connection that lie ahead when using these cards. In whatever form feels good to you, thank you Spirit team for the help, support, and guidance that is to come. If you are unsure how to invite or thank your Spirit team, please know it just needs to come from the heart. Remember, the greatest prayer that we can offer Spirit is a heartfelt "*Thank You!*" And so it is!

How to do
an Oracle Reading

1. **Get Grounded and Centered**. Being grounded is an essential step for those that are highly sensitive and pick up emotions from the people and the energy around them. Being grounded means you are present in your body and that you feel centered and balanced no matter what is happening around you. A simple way that I like to do this is by imagining a white light coming down from the heavens and entering my crown, traveling down to my heart. Then, I visualize roots – like roots of a tree – going from my feet down to the center of the earth until I feel connected. I take a couple of deep breaths and focus on my heart until I feel the balance between heaven and earth. Once I do, I am ready for the reading.

2. **Clear the cards.** There are many ways to do this. Some people put a crystal stone on top of the card deck, oftentimes **selenite**. This is to release any old energy from the cards. Some run the cards through the smoke of **sage** or **incense**.

I do this by inviting my Spirit Team in and saying a prayer or blessing. The prayer can be in whatever form feels right to you. I usually say something like, *"Angels, Guides and Loved Ones, I open my energy and heart to you today and I ask for your support and guidance during this reading for the highest greatest good of all concerned. I ask for truth, love, and guidance as I channel the energy of Spirit through me to _____ today. Thank you, and so it is."* Doing this clears the energy of the card deck and brings in support from the Spirit world. It also helps you get intentional with your own energy. I never do a reading without doing this.

3. **Ask a question or set an intention.** Be as clear and specific as possible about what you want guidance on today. You may set an intention such as, *"What message do I need to receive for my highest good today?"* or *"What guidance serves my highest good right now?"* If you are asking a question, it could be *"What do I need to know about _____ situation?"* or *"What guidance do I need to see the situation with _____ more clearly?"* Be clear about what you want guidance on, unless you are just wanting a message for the day.

4. **Shuffle your cards.** Shuffle the cards until you feel complete. There is no right amount of time. Just follow your guidance. As you are shuffling the cards, focus on the energy of your intention or

question. Then, you can cut the deck if you feel guided. Many people like to cut the deck three times and then put them all in a pile. This is up to you and does not need to be done, but certainly can be a part of your process. Do whatever feels right to you. Pay special attention to any cards that "fly" out of the deck. Those generally have special meaning and I always use those in addition to whatever spread I am reading. Those cards that "fly out" are usually significant… they won't wait until they are picked – so special attention is paid to those.

5. **Spread the cards.** I suggest that when you spread out your cards, you run your hands over them – kind of like hovering over them – until you feel a pull. When you feel that pull, then choose that card. If you are doing a reading for someone else, I have them hover their hand over the cards and ask them to pick the cards they are drawn to. I usually tell them how many cards to choose, based on the spread I am feeling guided to do for them. I like to use these words: "*Place your hands over the cards and choose whatever card you are drawn to.*" They often ask how they will know which card to pick. I ask them to pay attention to what they feel, see, hear, or know… and that their intuition will guide them to the right cards. Again, you can do a single card spread, or select several cards, depending on what

your guidance says or what spread you choose to do.

6. **Tune into the card(s).** Once you've pulled a card or multiple cards, let your intuition guide you to the meaning for you or the person you are reading for. Don't rush to the guidebook. Feel into the cards. Look at the images. Listen to the messages that may come with them. Pay attention to the thoughts that come to you. This lets your intuition and your Spirit Team connect with you to offer you the complete message. Remember, the messages will come to you through your five senses, so be mindful of all of them. Observe how your body feels and what it might be telling you, especially if you are doing your own reading. You may also want to share that with the person you are doing the reading for so they can become aware of how their body is responding as well. Give your intuition a chance. Be sure to notice any consistent themes, words, phrases, or symbols that show up in the cards. What images, words, sounds, or feelings come up as you read them? Maybe you had that inner knowing or memory about something? Take it all in. Oftentimes, by being open to receive the profound messages that show up, this will begin a healing process that opens the door to changes in your life or the life of the person you are reading for.

7. **Look in the guidebook, if needed.** Now, if guided, you can go to the information in the guidebook to confirm or validate what you felt when first reading the cards. Oftentimes the message in the guidebook can help you expand your own interpretation as well.

8. **Give Thanks!** In whatever form feels good to you, thank your Spirit team and the person you are reading for as well. Again, if you are unsure how thank your Spirit team, please know, it just needs to come from the heart. Remember, the greatest prayer that we can offer Spirit is a heartfelt *"Thank You!"*

Ethics for
Oracle Card Readers

Intuition

You've read all kinds of books and taken classes to develop your intuition. Sometimes, you see a card, and it feels different to you than what it usually does. It may represent a different energy, or the message feels completely different. I find this happens when you begin to expand beyond the cards. Your intuition is growing.

Always, and in all ways, listen to your gut and deliver the message that comes to you. Don't be limited by the words on the card. Don't ignore your intuition. Ask for clarity – maybe draw another card – but always listen to your intuition and share that with the person you are reading for. Don't go against your intuition. Go with it and let the reading unfold naturally.

Respect

Respect your cards and the energy they carry. If you aren't taking the reading seriously, the cards will show that and will not be a fit for the person. You must respect the cards, yourself as a reader, and the person receiving the reading. By following the above steps and creating sacred space for your readings you are already showing respect.

You can have boundaries and decide to read only for those that take it seriously. Don't read for people who put it down or want to make it a joke. Some people will want you to read their cards, but believe that they are BS. You do not need to read for those that are not in the energy YOU choose to bring into your space. Many people that show up in an energy that doesn't feel respectful are actually just scared or insecure. Use your intuition to decide who you want to read for and when.

Honesty

When you read oracle cards for someone, know that you are the messenger. Give the message exactly as it comes to you. Always be honest, but don't be brutal or judgmental. You are not the one to decide what that message means for the person or the actions to take. Oracle cards are tools for guidance above all else. They are not definitive. In each card, you can find a variety of meanings, so be mindful when sharing how it's showing up for their particular reading. In difficult situations, remember that free will exists, always. Anytime there is a problem, there is also always more than one solution. Remind the person you are reading for of this in those hard readings.

Trust

Building trust with the person you are reading for goes hand-in-hand with being ethical. They are coming to you because they have a challenge, some more serious than others. It is your responsibility to be authentic, kind, helpful, and truthful. Don't say things to try and make them feel better … or to make them feel bad. Nothing is ever as black and white as we see it, especially from Spirit's perspective. Assure them that by listening to their own inner guidance they have the ability to direct their free will energy and expand beyond today's challenge.

It is important to remember that people are putting their trust and faith in you. With that, they often give you their power. This is something that you cannot stop them from doing, but you can help them be aware that their power is in *their* hands, not yours. I believe there is a great responsibility as a reader to honor the power of the person you are reading for and help them to help themselves with the guidance and support that comes from the reading. Also, don't try and diagnose someone who has health or mental health problems; but instead, help support them on the emotional and spiritual level while directing them towards a medical professional as well.

It's common sense, but it is important to remember that there are many vulnerable people in the world. There are also many unethical people using the titles of psychic or oracle card reader to take advantage of those people and instead line their pockets. Having compassion in your heart and offering them the guidance and truth they deserve are the best things you can do to support them... and humanity.

A Note about Guidebooks

There is no one right way to prepare your cards, just like there is no one road to spirituality. There are many ways, and you will find your own way through a combination of techniques you see and hear about as you journey through the years. That is the best way – to follow your innate knowing. I will share with you my way… and trust that you will find your way with practice and development of your own natural intuition.

One of the ways to deepen your understanding of reading oracle cards is by practicing your readings without using a guidebook. When you rely on your own intuition by tuning into the images, the words, and listening to your gut instincts, you will begin to experience how your intuition supports you in discerning the guidance that is coming through the cards. When you always rely on the guidebook for meaning, you will always need a guidebook. When you are first starting out, or are new to a deck, using the guidebook here and there is fine. You are settling into the energy of the cards and your intuition. The real growth occurs when you can set the guidebook aside and follow your own intuition on what Spirit is telling you.

When looking at oracle card images and words, the reader can tune into a lot more information when they connect with their heart and let intuition guide them to the messages. Guidebooks can only go so far in answering a question – but the reader can really tune in and go deep – pulling the most appropriate, resonate answers from within. This is why experienced teachers like me suggest you follow your intuition FIRST; then if you must, look to the guidebook SECOND, to support or validate the messages you received.

When you are stumped by a card and the message it is sharing with you, instead of consulting the guidebook, I would suggest you first ask Spirit for clarity and pull another card from the oracle deck. This will help you expand your abilities and develop more trust within yourself. If, after asking for clarity, you still feel stuck or unsure, consult the guidebook.

Remember, oracle cards are a tool for guidance and self-reflection to add to your spiritual practice. They can be used to tune into a situation or experience you are having, to provide guidance and direction, as well as comfort or support. Oracle cards are only the tool. Your intuition is the key. The cards help you hone your intuitive skills and develop a trust for yourself and your ability to intuit and interpret the messages you are receiving.

TIPS FOR USING ORACLE CARDS

There aren't many rules when it comes to working with these divination tools, but here are a few things to keep in mind as you move forward on your Oracle Card journey:

1. **Your oracle cards are sacred.** You can use a deck for years and it can be well-worn and well-loved, but be sure they are respected as the sacred tool that they are.

2. **Don't rely on the guidebook.** Those of us that create oracle cards put a lot of time and love into the cards as well as these guidebooks. It can be fun and informative to read the entries when you get a new deck. However, as I have mentioned before, your intuition is what we want to rely on. So, when you read the words, don't pay as much attention to the longer explanation of the card in the guidebook and instead listen to what your own intuition is telling you this card means for you right now, at this time in your life.

3. **Pay attention to the images and the energy as much as the words.** The images on oracle cards are beautiful, but they aren't just pretty pictures. There is energy and intention behind each one. Different cards have different layers of meanings. Therefore, the words on the card may not resonate with you, but the image might. For example, an image of a particular angel or guide might remind you of a vision you had days earlier... or an image of an animal might remind you of a beloved pet.

4. **Be open to receive.** Intense emotions can block your intuition. Anxiety and fear can hold you back from seeing clearly. So, stay open and focused, but also relax and have fun. The lighter and higher your energy is, the clearer the messages will be. Remember that these cards help you to get in touch with your Higher Self and your Spirit Team. Oracle cards can be startlingly accurate. It is Spirit's way of communicating with you. Staying open and letting go of the uncertainty or disbelief will help you get even more out of your readings.

5. **Pay attention to upside-down cards.** When you or the person you are doing the reading for picks an upside-down card, I suggest not turning it the right way, but leaving it exactly the way the cards are drawn naturally. There is a

special meaning there. In traditional tarot, it is taught that it is a reversal card, therefore it means the opposite of what the card says. I don't subscribe to that belief. The way I look at upside-down cards is different. I see that whatever the focus of the card is, it is in motion; but something, internal or external, is holding it back or slowing down the progress. It also means to me that the message of this card is meant to stand out. It is being highlighted.

6. **Don't use oracle cards as a crutch.** When you feel the need to ask the same questions repeatedly, it is a sign of insecurity in the answers and/or your ability to tune in. It shows Spirit that you aren't trusting the messages you are receiving. Which, in the beginning, you may not; however, keep showing up and you'll get better at discerning the messages. Developing your intuition takes practice. There is no need to ask several times a day; in fact, I wouldn't advise it.

Keep practicing and you will find a rhythm that works for you. Maybe you do a reading once a week, pull a card every morning, or at the end your day with a message to take you into your sleep. You'll find a frequency that works for you. It's less important about the number of times you do a reading as it is to be open, connected, and clear. Remember, the cards are just the tools to tap into your innate wisdom. It is YOU ultimately that is the oracle. Trust yourself and trust the oracle.

Rules You May Hear About Oracle Cards – Decide What Feels True for You

I don't follow these rules, however, I wanted to share them with you in case you have heard of them or have any fear around not following them. I believe it is helpful to know some of the "beliefs" that people have around Oracle cards, as they often get mentioned when this topic comes up. As with everything, **listen to your guidance**. If it feels right, do it; if it doesn't, don't.

1. When doing a reading for someone else, do not let the person you are reading for touch your cards. You should be the only person shuffling and picking the cards, that way no one else touches your deck.

2. When you're done pulling cards, keep your deck in a closed drawer so it doesn't pick up on stray vibes flying around your home.

3. Keep your cards wrapped in red silk to keep them safe from negative energy.

ORACLE CARD SPREADS

There are many different cards spreads you can use for an oracle card reading. I am including a few of my favorites. Some spreads go back to the traditional Tarot, which I have not included here.

As with everything else, listen to your guidance. Sometimes when I do a reading, I ask my Spirit Team how many cards I should choose (or how many cards the person I am reading for needs to choose) and I read them that way. Sometimes the number of cards just pops into my head, so I go with that. Oftentimes, I ask the person I am reading for if a number comes to their mind, and I have them go with that number.

Practice all of these examples and spreads and see which ones you enjoy best. You may pick different spreads for different people or specific areas of focus. Let your intuition guide you.

The Past - Present - Future Spread

THE PAST - PRESENT - FUTURE SPREAD

Choose 3 cards - Lay the first one down, then the next one to the right of that, and the third one to the right of that.

The first card to your left is the recent past, the middle card is the current present situation, and the one to the right is the outcome or future.

7-Card Spread - Chakra Reading

7 CARD SPREAD - CHAKRA READING

Choose 7 cards - Lay the first one to your far left, and each one after that to its right. Each card in the order of 1 – 7 (with 1 being the 1st card on your left, 2 being the second, and so on) tells about certain aspects of your life dealing with the specific chakras and their areas as mentioned below.

1 - **Root Chakra**: Security, home, safety, self-reliance, desire for life.

2 - **Sacral Chakra**: Attitudes, feeling accepted, body, sex, kinship, belonging to a group.

3 - **Solar Plexus Chakra**: Emotions, personal power, control, health, intellectual ability.

4 - **Heart Chakra**: Love & romance, prosperity, circulation, expanded feelings of relationship to all.

5 - **Throat Chakra**: Speaking out, creativity, making yourself known, communication.

6 - **3rd Eye Chakra**: Being seen for who you are, taking charge of your thoughts.

7 - **Crown Chakra**: Serving the highest good, manifesting vision.

The One Year Spread

Choose 12 cards - Lay them out from left to right in the order that you choose them. The first card on the left represents the current month, and the following month next, and so on.

Single Card Reading

SINGLE CARD READING

Choose one card as your theme for the day or a message from the angels just for today.

Looking Ahead Spread

LOOKING AHEAD SPREAD

Ask the Question: *"What is coming up for me?"* or *"What do the next three months look like?"*

Choose 3 cards - The first card is your present, the second card is the immediate future 1-2 months ahead, and the third card is 2-3 months ahead.

A BRAND-NEW
ORACLE CARD DECK

I have recently created a brand-new Oracle Card deck: **The Multi-Dimensional Oracle cards.**

These cards were channeled with Love, Intention, Light, and Possibilities. The cards called me to them. They were intentionally channeled through me, guiding me to the artist, Lucinda Rae, in an effortless and Divine way.

The energy of Love came through me as each Oracle announced themselves.

There was clear Intention throughout the entire creation of this deck: from the beginning idea to the project completion. I could feel the Light manifest as each card came into visual creation.

With the LOVE, INTENTION and LIGHT... came the great gift this Multi-Dimensional Oracle deck has to offer: **POSSIBILITIES**.

The possibility that you will begin to connect with and trust your intuition and not depend on what others tell you. The possibility that you recognize that your true nature is Spirit first and foremost and you choose to expand beyond the training of our 3D world. The possibility that you are opening up to the Numbers, Symbols, Animals, and Ascended Masters that are here to support and guide you... the very Multi-Dimensional You!

There is a vast amount of life to discover beyond this 3D world. **My vision is that these cards will help you to discover, connect, and rise to meet the guidance and support that the higher dimensions are waiting to share with you**. Oracle cards support your emotional and spiritual health by attuning you to a greater sense of inner knowledge, wisdom, and intuition.

The Multi-Dimensional Oracle is a tool that can help you remember and reconnect with your multi-dimensional self.

Welcome to the Multi-Dimensional Journey!

In Light,
Sunny Dawn Johnston

> Order your Multi-Dimensional
> Oracle Card deck today HERE:
>
> **https://multidimensionaloracle.cards/shop**

SUNNY DAWN JOHNSTON

Psychic Medium | Intuitive Teacher | Author |
Spiritual Biz Mentor

Sunny Dawn Johnston is an acclaimed psychic medium, changemaker, transformational thought leader, and spiritual biz mentor. She is the author of twenty books, including her flagship bestsellers, ***Invoking the Archangels*** and *The Love Never Ends*, which have become the cornerstones for many of her keynote topics such as intuition, mediumship, and the angelic realm.

Through her courses, private sessions, and live events, Sunny has grown and cultivated a diverse global community. Whether in-person or online, her strong mentorship encourages thousands of students to connect with their heart and the core of their being and guides them to experience life in a higher vibrational, multi-dimensional way.

Sunny is also the creator of the *ELEV8 Your Life* membership site… a virtual community focused on designing a high-vibrational life – bursting with abundance, self-love, and joy. Leading the ELEV8 Your Life community, Sunny focuses on accountability, support, and guidance as the solid foundation of intentional and lasting transformation. All are welcome to join ELEV8 Your Life, where members have exclusive access to 20+ years of her knowledge and teachings.

Sunny's biz membership, *My Spiritual Biz*, is a community for heart-based entrepreneurs. Sunny's 30 years of business experience and her multi-million dollar generating team guide and mentor members who are starting, building, or growing a spirit-based business. Sunny and her team of experts provide the bridge between envisioning and actualizing your entrepreneurial dreams.

SDJ Productions has expanded Sunny's work beyond writing and speaking engagements and into publishing books, CD's, and oracle card decks. Her latest project is *The Multi-Dimensional Oracle Card Deck.* Sunny believes it is time to embrace ALL of our BE-ingness … and to do that, we must let go of what we have been taught about living in this 3D reality. There is so much more, and it is calling us to ascend, expand and embrace our multi-dimensional reality. She is on a mission to help others connect and align with the true power of their being as well.

In her spare time, Sunny is actively involved in the spiritual community and volunteers as a psychic investigator for the international organization FIND ME. This is a non-profit organization of Psychic, Investigative, and Canine Search & Rescue (SAR) volunteers collaborating to support law enforcement and families of missing persons and homicide victims.

Check out more info on Sunny at:
https://sunnydawnjohnston.com

Check out my **Sunny Dawn Johnston online events calendar** on my website and join me for my next Oracle Card Bootcamp to do a deep dive into Oracle Cards … and order your Multi-Dimensional Oracle Card deck here today:
https://multidimensionaloracle.cards/shop

ORACLE CARD BOOTCAMP

As a psychic medium, I know how important it is to learn to trust your intuition. Before I started doing my work professionally, I struggled with the confidence to accept that this was my gift and to share it with others. I knew I was meant to support others in learning and growing spiritually, but I wasn't sure what that looked like. I had been using oracle cards for myself and loved them. They were a great bridge between my own intuition and the guidance and messages from the Spirit world. The cards helped me to trust what was coming through and to share it. As my confidence grew, I realized that the cards were validating what I already knew. They had given me the confidence to trust my intuition for my own personal life as well as to trust it for those that were looking for guidance. That's when I started to do readings professionally. After a couple of years, I discovered that I no longer needed the cards for readings. They were a tool that I had outgrown, and I stopped using them for readings.

However, as I have mentioned before, I had a love for oracle cards. So, even though I stopped using them professionally, I continued using them for myself: pulling a card every morning, going to the cards when struggling with a decision, and sometimes using them to validate my own guidance on a BIG business change.

As you have already learned, oracle cards and divination tools have been a part of history for as long as people have wanted to connect with the great unknown, the Spirit World. There is so much to learn and expand into – and the cards are a powerful and fun way to do that.

If you are new to oracle cards, or are seasoned in them, there is always more to learn. As a student of Spirit, I have found that learning at different times, with different people and tools, can truly expand your growth and intuition. So, if you are ready to DIVE into Oracle Cards, expand your knowledge and experience, and TUNE IN to your INNNATE WISDOM, this Oracle Card Bootcamp is for you! This 3-hour workshop will also include plenty of LIVE Q&A time with me. You will have the opportunity to practice with your own card deck as well, so have yours handy. Let's work together to open up to your intuition, expand your awareness, and tune into the oracles. Come and join me for our next Oracle Card Bootcamp!

Oracle Card Bootcamp with Sunny Dawn Johnston

Online via Zoom; class will be recorded for your convenience.

Login details will be sent with your registration confirmation.

Date & Time: Details available at the link below.

REGISTRATION LINK:

https://events.sunnydawnjohnston.com/events/oracle-card-bootcamp

CONNECT WITH SUNNY

 Calendar of Events

Check out all my classes, workshops, retreats, online events, and travel opportunities https://events.sunnydawnjohnston.com

Ongoing Support

SDJ S.O.U.L. (Spiritual Online Universal Learning) - *Home of all my Online Learning!*

Check out my online courses that have been created with the intention of YOU, the participant, walking through them step-by-step, in your own time and space. Each course is based on one of my books and/or one of my live online courses, so they are all proven to be very impactful and full of great nuggets of information. **https://sdjsoul.com**

 **Off the Cuff podcast:**

Sunny talks with people about everyday life, from the spiritual, the physical and the metaphysical perspective every weekday at 1:11pm PACIFIC time (2:11pm MT, 3:11pm CT, 4:11pm ET)

LIVE!!! Simulcast on **Sunny's Facebook Fan page:** https://www.facebook.com/SunnyDawnJohnstonFanPage

Off the Cuff (recorded): https://sunnydawnjohnston.com/podcasts

 <u>Membership Communities</u>

Spirit Speaks LIVE!

Join my *SPIRIT SPEAKS LIVE!* monthly membership event for your ONLINE opportunity to ask your questions, raise your vibration into alignment with the Spirit world, and find out what Spirit wants you to know. These insightful hour-long group sessions will bring you clarity, comfort, confidence and even creativity in the moment! **Join live ONLINE** the second Wednesday of every month at 5pm Pacific. https://sdjsoul.com/spiritspeaks

ELEV8 Your Life

Community support & mentoring – All Year Long

An *ELEV8 Your Life* Membership is your sanctuary for healing, transforming, ascending…

Become a member of this like-hearted community and live a higher-vibrational life every day! ELEV8 open enrollment occurs several times a year. **Join our Waitlist** to be the first to know when the next Open Enrollment occurs. **https://elev8yourlife.love**

My Spiritual Biz

Your Entrepreneurial Headquarters for Consistent Heart-Based Support & Dedication to Your Success. Whether you already have a business and aren't sure how to scale it or you want to turn that pastime into a profit-generating machine, *My Spiritual Biz* is the place for expansion. The Universe is beckoning you to step up, open up, co-create, and receive … and my team and I are here to support YOU in doing just that! **Join now** for Live, Interactive Weekly Support from Sunny Dawn Johnston and her Multi-Million Dollar Generating Team. **https://myspiritualbiz.com**

Media Connections

Follow me on these Social Media platforms:

- **Facebook Fan Page**:
  https://www.facebook.com/SunnyDawnJohnstonFanPage
- **SDJ Community Facebook group**:
  https://www.facebook.com/groups/SDJCommunity
- **Instagram**:
  https://www.instagram.com/sunnydawn.johnston/
- **YouTube**:
  https://www.youtube.com/user/sunnydawnjohnston

Radio Stations

 BE the Change online streaming radio station:

24/7 free access every day of the week with inspiring talk and music

https://sunnydawnjohnston.com/radio or download the iPhone or Android app for mobile

Looking forward to connecting with you soon!